Plans for small gardens 2

Cover: a delightful cottage garden, showing the effectiveness of 'gardening without grass' (photograph by Harry Smith Horticultural Photographic Collection)

Overleaf: shade is a common problem in small gardens, but may be overcome with the right choice of plants (see p. 13)

Plans for small gardens 2

A Wisley Handbook

Geoffrey K. Coombs

Cassell

The Royal Horticultural Society

Cassell Educational Limited
Artillery House
Artillery Row
London, SW1P 1RT
for the Royal Horticultural Society

First published 1987

British Library Cataloguing in Publication Data

Coombs, Geoffrey K.
  Plans for small gardens 2.
  1. Gardening
  II. Title   II. Royal Horticultural Society
  III. Series
  635   SB450.97

  ISBN 0-304-31147-2

Photographs by Michael Warren and the Harry Smith
Collection.
Design by Lesley Stewart.

Phototypesetting by Chapterhouse, Formby
Printed in Hong Kong by Wing King Tong Co. Ltd

Contents

Introduction

This book is a sequel to *Plans for small gardens*, published in the same series. It is written particularly for the many people with small to medium-sized gardens, although the needs of gardeners with larger sites, up to an acre or more, have also been taken into consideration. However, the designs are 'elastic' in the sense that they can be adapted to different gardens, whatever the size and shape.

The book aims both to inspire and to solve problems. It includes plans for a herb garden – now very popular with gardeners – and advice on how to deal with an awkward slope or a garden in shade. Lists of suitable plants are given according to situation, together with suggested colour combinations and other ideas such as introducing scented flowers. The main emphasis throughout is on gardens which can be easily maintained, with the minimum amount of time and labour.

Below: an interesting combination of brick and paving for a patio

Opposite: a new garden with a bed of dwarf conifers and heathers which will be easy to maintain (see also p. 45)

Some preliminaries

Whether starting with a bare site or changing an existing garden, the order of work should be based on a definite programme. This will include clearing, levelling and drainage and, if it involves moving heavy material, should be completed before more delicate operations such as laying the lawn are carried out. It is sensible to construct paths and paved areas at an early stage to improve access and, when it comes to making the lawn, this can be raised slightly above the paving, which facilitates mowing.

If sowing a lawn, it is a good idea to place a single line of turf

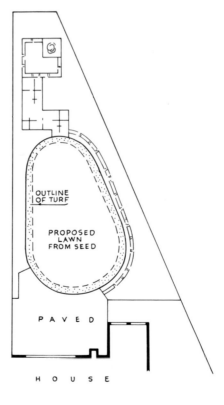

Figure 1: a line of turf round the perimeter of a newly sown lawn gives a firm edge immediately

Elaeagnus pungens 'Maculata' makes a fine evergreen hedge,
particularly when interspersed with clematis and climbing roses

round the entire perimeter of the area (see figure 1). This is particularly useful on light sandy soil where the edges of the lawn may
be slow to consolidate. It gives a very satisfactory immediate
outline, so that the garden looks as if it is taking shape, and within
a few days allows one to cut a firm neat edge round the newly
sown lawn. It is more economical to divide each piece of turf
lengthwise in half, which is still wide enough for the purpose.

Hedges or other screens, flower beds and paths are three of the
most important basic items in a design. Hedges used for division
(as opposed to boundary hedges) help to give structure to a
garden, although the expense of planting them is sometimes
begrudged. They provide a background for the plants in front of
them, just as walls enclose and complement the decor of a room.
An evergreen hedge which might be thought sombre and dull can
be interspersed with sections of square trellis of the same height
and roses or shrubs can be trained against it to introduce colour
(see figure 2 overleaf).

Hedges sometimes create competitive root problems. Privet is a
notorious offender and the roots spread over a wide area, particularly when close to a bed that has been dug and manured.
Fortunately, many of the old privet hedges which were so
common in front and back gardens have been replaced. However,

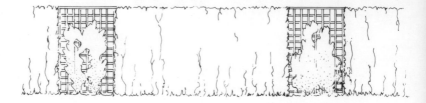

Figure 2: a hedge line broken with sections of trellis against which shrubs or roses can be trained

those that remain can be controlled by digging a narrow trench to a depth of about 2 feet (60 cm), 1 to 1½ feet (30–45 cm) away from the base, and burying pieces of old plastic or corrugated iron (often obtainable as scrap from a builder). These should be placed level with or just below the ground and will be completely hidden when the trench is filled in (see figure 3). Lilac, a close relative of privet, and other invasive shrubs which impoverish the soil around them, can be treated in a similar way. The trench should be dug 1 to 2 feet (30–60 cm) from the stems and will enable the bed to be manured without the widespreading shrubs receiving most of the benefit.

Paths and paved areas open up many variations in design and, with old material put to new use, concrete is now an ingredient in many products. Concrete bricks and small slabs (known as setts) lend themselves to sweeping fluid curves and circles around features such as a modern sculpture or urn. Paving stones or concrete can be laid as a garden path, say 3 feet (90 cm) wide, and the squares edged with grey or reddish bricks, which combine well with the colours, to make an interesting pattern and texture.

For further information about basic design and planning, see the introduction to *Plans for small gardens*.

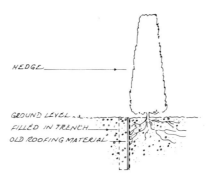

Figure 3: old roofing material buried to prevent roots spreading

A front garden

The layout of the garden in front of a house is not always taken to its full potential and yet it is supposed to be the first welcoming introduction to the home. The approach to the house, from the moment of crossing the boundary, should leave no doubt about the direction of the front door. The commonest and most regrettable mistake is to have an impressive expanse of concrete or asphalt leading towards the garage and a small insignificant path at right angles going to the house. The path should be as wide and spacious as possible within the proportions of the garden, creating a feeling of being drawn towards the front entrance.

The garden in plan 1 was designed with these requirements in mind. The paving slabs are set in a scree of shingle, into which rock plants and a few heathers may be planted with charming effect. The entrance to the garage cannot be overlooked, even if it

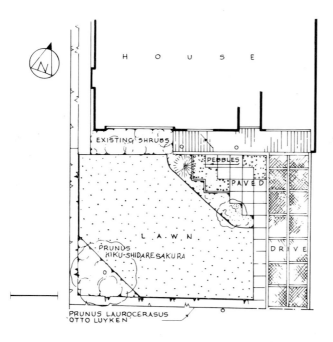

Plan 1: a front garden, using several materials to produce different textures

A mixture of paving and shingle dotted with low-growing plants

is not the most aesthetic feature of the garden. However, a large area of hard material can be improved by using bricks to make square divisions infilled with paving, concrete setts or textured concrete (see also p. 10). Another example of this technique is given in plan 5 (p. 22), which shows the forecourt of a listed building. It has been designed to include a parking space, using bricks similar in colour to the house to make the intrusion of modern necessities more acceptable. Paving is inlaid between the brick divisions, which measure 4 by 4 feet (1.2×1.2 m).

A garden in shade

A large number of our garden plants have been introduced from other parts of the world and most are remarkably tolerant of the vagaries of the British climate. Some are particularly useful, delighting in more open parts of the garden but being not averse to shaded positions.

There are various degrees of shade. While many plants, such as border phlox, erigeron, hosta, aquilegia and certain roses, are happy on the north side of a wall, the choice is much more selective under a close covering of trees, where the soil is often dry and impoverished by the roots. Even the density of the tree canopy varies and plants which might grow perfectly well beneath the light open branches of a false acacia will not survive under the thick foliage of a sycamore. The nature of the soil, whether acid or alkaline, dry or moist, is also critical.

Plan 2 (p. 15) represents an imaginary garden in three possible combinations of shade and soil type, with three tables of appropriate plants corresponding to these different situations. Table 1 gives plants that should succeed in total shade in slightly alkaline or neutral soil. More usually, however, one or other side of the garden receives a limited amount of sun and table 2 therefore lists plants suitable for partial shade. In these more favourable conditions, a number of colourful shrubs can be recommended to replace some of the more sombre evergreens and groups of naturalized bulbs, such as aconites, snowdrops and chionodoxa, could be established between the larger plants.

Table 3 is a planting scheme for moist acid soil in semi-shade and includes rhododendrons, azaleas and hydrangeas. Hortensia and lacecap hydrangeas resent dryness at the roots and will revel in such a situation, producing their flowerheads in shades of blue and purple. Table 4 contains suggested plants for dense shade under trees.

Overleaf above: the colourful long-spurred *Aquilegia* hybrids flower in early summer and seed themselves freely (see table 2, p. 16)

Overleaf below: *Camellia japonica* 'Magnoliiflora', a beautiful medium-sized shrub of compact habit, will thrive in semi-shade on acid or neutral soil (see table 3, p. 16)

Plan 2:   a garden in shade, illustrating three different conditions of
shade

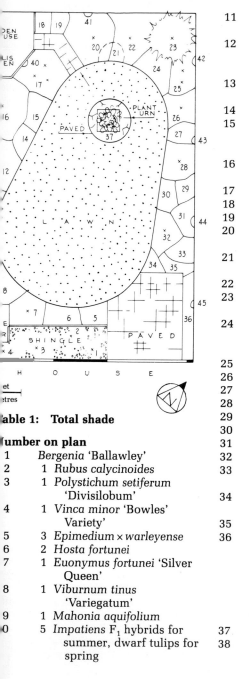

11   3 *Epimedium grandiflorum*
      'Rose Queen'
12   1 *Sarcococca confusa* and 5
      Lamium maculatum
      'Beacon Silver'
13   3 *Anemone* × *hybrida*
      'September Charm'
14   3 *Tiarella wherryi*
15   7 *Impatiens* F$_1$ hybrids for
      summer, dwarf tulips for
      spring
16   1 *Elaeagnus* × *ebbingei* 'Gilt
      Edge'
17   3 *Viburnum davidii*
18   1 *Brunnera microphylla*
19   1 *Iris foetidissima*
20   1 *Aucuba japonica*
      'Crotonifolia'
21   3 *Cyclamen purpurascens*
      (*C.europaeum*)
22   1 *Laurus nobilis*
23   1 *Cephalotaxus harringtonia*
      'Fastigiata'
24   9 *Impatiens* F$_1$ hybrids for
      summer, dwarf tulips for
      spring
25   2 *Mahonia aquifolium*
26   1 *Skimmia* × *foremanii*
27   3 *Astrantia major*
28   1 *Daphne lanceolata*
29   1 *Helleborus lividus corsicus*
30   1 *Geranium macrorrhizum*
31   3 *Brunnera microphylla*
32   1 *Danae racemosa*
33   3 *Anemone* × *hybrida*
      'Bressingham Glow'
34   3 *Tellima grandiflora*
      'Purpurea'
35   9 *Impatiens* F$_1$ hybrids
36   3 *Viola odorata*
      3 *Asarum caudatum*
      3 *Cyclamen hederifolium*
      3 *Cyclamen hederifolium*
      'Album'
      3 *Pulmonaria rubra* 'Bowles'
      Variety'
37   1 *Fatsia japonica*
38   1 *Hedera colchica* 'Dentata
      Variegata'

Table 1:   Total shade

Number on plan

1   *Bergenia* 'Ballawley'
2   1 *Rubus calycinoides*
3   1 *Polystichum setiferum*
      'Divisilobum'
4   1 *Vinca minor* 'Bowles'
      Variety'
5   3 *Epimedium* × *warleyense*
6   2 *Hosta fortunei*
7   1 *Euonymus fortunei* 'Silver
      Queen'
8   1 *Viburnum tinus*
      'Variegatum'
9   1 *Mahonia aquifolium*
10   5 *Impatiens* F$_1$ hybrids for
      summer, dwarf tulips for
      spring

39	1 climbing rose 'Madam Alfred Carrière'
40	1 *Jasminum nudiflorum*
41	1 climbing rose 'Mermaid'
42	1 *Hedera helix* 'Glacier'
43	1 *Jasminum nudiflorum*
44	1 climbing rose 'Zephirine Drouhin'
45	1 *Choisya ternata*

Table 2: Partial shade

Number on plan

1	(see table 1 where no name is given)
2	
3	
4	
5	
6	3 *Fuchsia* 'Alice Hoffmann'
7	
8	
9	1 *Daphne retusa*
10	
11	
12	1 *Mahonia japonica*
13	
14	
15	
16	
17	3 hybrid musk roses 'Penelope'
18	
19	
20	1 *Ilex × altaclerense* 'Golden King'
21	
22	
23	
24	5 bush floribunda (cluster-flowered) roses 'Dearest'
25	1 *Weigela florida* 'Variegata'
26	
27	3 *Astilbe × arendsii* 'Fire'
28	3 hybrid musk roses 'Felicia'
29	
30	
31	5 *Aquilegia* long-spurred hybrids
32	1 *Chaenomeles speciosa* 'Simonii'

33	1 *Fuchsia* 'Mrs Popple'
34	
35	9 *Begonia semperflorens*
36	
37	
38	1 *Pyracantha* 'Watereri'
39	1 climbing rose 'Golden Showers'
40	1 *Pyracantha* 'Golden Dome'
41	
42	
43	1 *Cotoneaster lacteus*

Table 3: Partial shade and acid soil

Number on plan

1	1 *Andromeda polifolia* 'Compacta'
2	1 *Gaultheria procumbens*
3	(see table 1 where no name is given)
4	
5	
6	3 *Fuchsia* 'Alice Hoffmann'
7	
8	1 *Rhododendron* 'Doncaster'
9	1 *Daphne retusa*
10	
11	
12	3 *Rhododendron* Exbury hybrids
13	
14	
15	
16	1 *Rhododendron* 'Mrs G. W. Leak'
17	3 *Hydrangea* 'Blue Wave'
18	
19	
20	
21	
22	1 *Hamamelis mollis*
23	1 *Laurus nobilis*
24	
25	2 *Rhododendron* 'Blaauw's Pink'
26	3 *Hydrangea* 'Lanarth White'
27	
28	1 *Camellia japonica* 'Magnoliiflora'
29	

A subtle blend of colours in the shade garden at Bressingham Hall, Norfolk

30
31 5 *Aquilegia* long-spurred
       hybrids
32 3 *Rhododendron*
       'Irohayama'
33 1 *Fuchsia* 'Mrs Popple'
34
35
36
37
38
39
40
41
42
43

Table 4:   Dense shade under trees

Arundinaria japonica
Arundinaria murielae
Aucuba japonica and cultivars
Buxus sempervirens
Fatsia japonica
Mahonia aquifolium
Rubus odoratus
Ruscus hypoglossum
Sarcococca confusa
Symphoricarpos × *chenaultii* 'Hancock'
Symphoricarpos × *doorenbosii* cultivars

A garden on a slope

A garden on a hill, with land either rising upward from the house or dropping away from it, has different problems to one on a level site. If the slope is gentle, the garden can probably be designed without altering the natural fall of the land, or a simple form of terracing could be undertaken which does not require excessive removal of earth, to produce a flat area of grass or paving.

However, for a garden on a steeper slope some consideration should be given to the heights and shapes of plants. As a general rule, where the ground rises from the viewpoint, it is preferable to have mostly fairly low plants, while on a downward incline, it is better to have tall plants in strategic places to avoid the feeling that the garden is slipping away. This can be seen most effectively on the hillsides in Italy, with narrow pencil-like cypresses appearing to almost peg the landscape in position.

Plan 3 illustrates a garden with a steep rise from the house to a more level section at the top, which is given over to a children's play area and space for growing vegetables and fruit. The original centre path has been replaced by a zig-zag path ascending from the lawn near the house and this forms a series of informal sloping terraces retained by low walls. The planting scheme in the centre part of the garden is based on low-growing plants and spreading shrubs, while larger plants are allowed at the sides and near the top to screen the vegetables and fruit. The paths are made of non-slip cream-coloured concrete setts and the patios in front of the house and summerhouse are of reconstituted rectangular paving.

The garden shown on plan 4 (p. 21) falls steeply to the lower boundary. It is rarely satisfactory for the garden to slope immediately away from the house and a flat level area should be made, even if it is relatively small, to provide a firm safe place for sitting and viewing the garden. The curved retaining wall gives a structural outline to the design and grass descends on each side to the lower lawn. Several small mature fruit trees have been kept to create much needed height and along the lower boundary a number of medium-sized conifers and eucalyptus will form an evergreen screen of varied texture and colour. Eucalyptus responds well to pruning every two years to restrict height and encourage thick bushy growth.

The shape of the lawn results in beds of different widths,

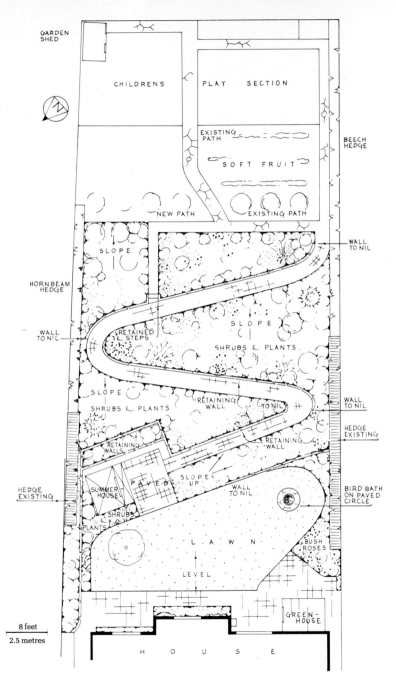

Plan 3: a garden on a slope inclining upward from the house

An example of successful planting in a hillside garden

offering scope for imaginative planting with plants that require various situations, whether cool shade or full sun. The continuous line around the lawn detracts from the actual boundaries, while the sundial makes a focal point of interest and gives depth to the design.

Large banks in awkward situations present a special problem. Here, as I have recommended before, climbing plants are very valuable in providing a cover, enabling one to dispense with grass and the need to cut it. The plants are spaced about 4 feet (1.2 m) apart near the top of the bank and allowed to ramble without support, quickly forming a dense cascading mat. A shrub that immediately comes to mind is *Lonicera japonica* 'Halliana', a semi-evergreen honeysuckle with scented biscuit-coloured flowers, which will spread 15 to 20 feet (4.5–6 m). Similarly, *L. japonica* 'Aureoreticulata', a honeysuckle mainly grown for its

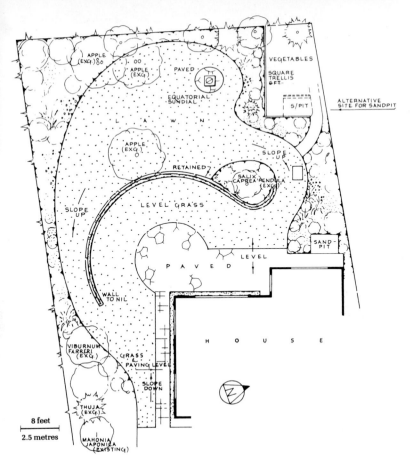

Plan 4: a garden on a slope falling away steeply from the house

variegated leaves, is excellent for the purpose. In places where other plants are reluctant to grow, *Hedera colchica* 'Dentata Variegata' might be the solution, either in shade under trees or in the open, and produces a carpet of large brightly variegated leaves over a wide area.

It may be almost impossible to actually plant in a very steep bank or cliff. However, many strong-growing climbers can be used in such a situation. They include *Polygonum baldschuanicum* (see p. 23), which should be planted away from trees; *Clematis montana* and its cultivars; *Parthenocissus quinquefolia*; and, in mild localities, *Meuhlenbeckia complexa*, which has delicate minute round leaves on thin wiry stems and will hang down like a curtain.

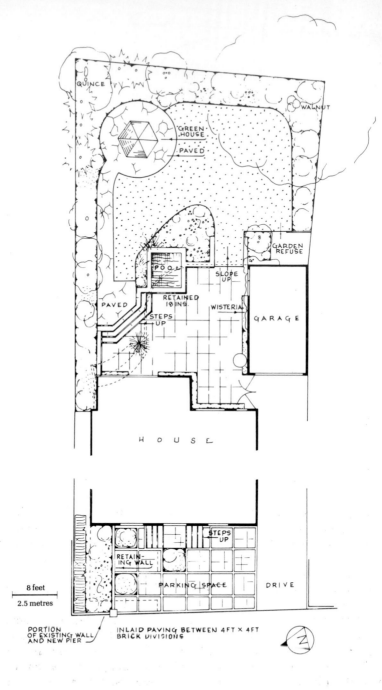

Plan 5: a garden on a slope rising from the house

22

Left: a curved retaining wall at the foot of a sloping bed

Right: the Russian vine, *Polygonum baldschuanicum*, is excellent for clothing a steep bank and flowers throughout summer and autumn

The garden in plan 5 is another site which slopes upwards from the house. The depth of gradient between the patio and the lawn is about 2 feet (60 cm), retained by a wall 1½ feet (45 cm) high. The steps are seen at an angle from the house on the left side of the garden, interrelating with the walling and the raised pool, and the greenhouse is an added feature to complete the picture. (The forecourt at the front of the house is mentioned on p. 12.)

An alternative to a lawn

It is often said that even in the smallest garden there should be room for a lawn, however tiny, and I am not advocating a reversal of this principle, nor suggesting that a lawn should be abandoned without careful reflection. However, there are certain circumstances where it may be impractical to maintain a lawn and where the possible alternatives should be considered.

In plan 6 (overleaf) the grass has been replaced with shingle, while access to different parts of the garden is provided by the paving. A gradual upwards slope away from the house leads to a terrace at the north end with chairs and a table, where the owner may take advantage of a few sunny hours. The thickness of the shingle scree depends on the size of the pebbles. Aggregate of up to ¾ inch (20 mm) could be laid to a depth of about 2 inches (5 cm), giving a pleasant textured effect with the paving. Larger stones are more difficult to walk on and cannot be tucked round the stems of plants rooted in the soil underneath.

It is important to ensure first that all weeds are eradicated from the site and the ground should be made level and consolidated by rolling or treading in the same way as when preparing a lawn. The actual planting is not difficult. Having decided on the planting positions, a small area of pebbles is removed and laid aside and the soil excavated to a depth of 9 to 10 inches (25 cm) and 12 inches (30 cm) wide, replacing it with prepared compost suitable for the requirements of the plant. This should also be mixed into the sides of the hole and into the natural soil at the bottom. The plants are then inserted and the pebbles replaced closely around them. This scree effect is relatively simple to achieve, compared with a proper scree bed specially designed for those choice flora which flourish in broken rock and debris. There is a fine example of this type of moraine in the new alpine house at the RHS Garden, Wisley.

Planting in the scree brings a soft informal theme to the garden. Shrubs like *Juniperus communis* 'Repanda', *Rubus calycinoides*

Above: scree beds at the Hillier Garden, Hampshire – an idea that can be easily adapted by the ordinary gardener

Below: a small pool fits nicely into an expanse of shingle and allows greater variety in planting (see p. 29)

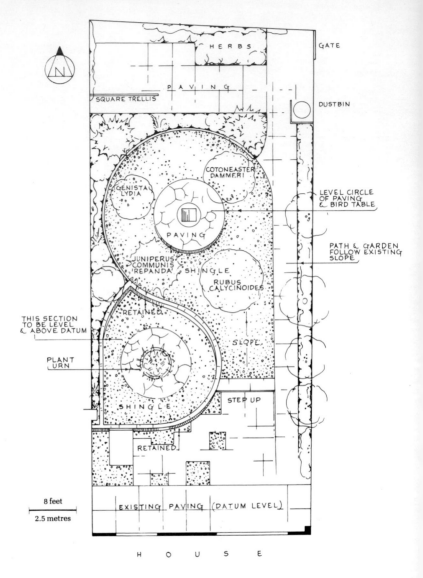

Plan 6:   an alternative to a lawn, with shrubs growing in shingle
scree

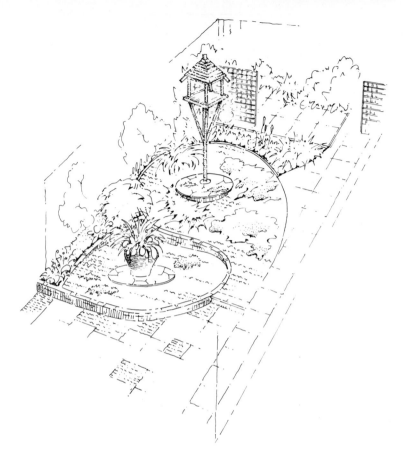

Sketch of the garden in plan 6

and *Cotoneaster dammeri* will grow through the pebbles and cover large sections with flat rug-like branches. Within a year or two the shingle will virtually disappear under closely knit steely grey and green foliage. Spreading rock plants, such as *Polygonum vacciniifolium*, *Dryas octopetala*, rock roses and thymes, can be inserted in the gaps. The adjacent beds are easily managed, planted with low perennials, small shrubs and dwarf bulbs and hardy cyclamen. A bold feature of flower and foliage is created with an urn on the lower terrace and the bird table near the centre of the garden provides another point of interest.

27

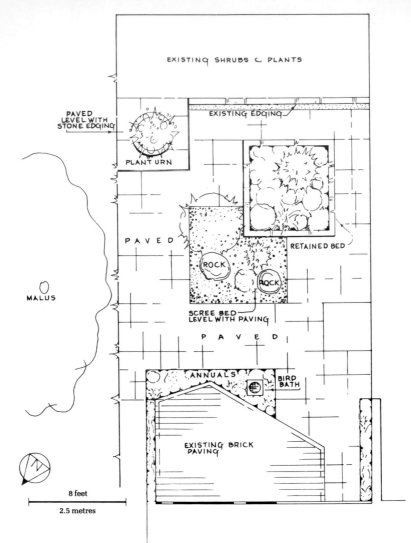

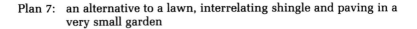

Plan 7: an alternative to a lawn, interrelating shingle and paving in a
very small garden

Plan 7 depicts a previously characterless small site which has
been improved by introducing an area of scree and different
levels with paving and a raised rectangular bed. The area round
the urn is about 6 inches (15 cm) high and the retained bed
approximately 10 inches (25 cm) high. It could easily be adapted to
include a larger section of shingle, with the paving reduced to

paths for walking across the garden. One or two well chosen rocks partly buried in the stones give a pleasing variation in texture and elevation, particularly if some carpeting plants are used around the base.

An alternative to the square bed would be a pool. This is best in sun, which most aquatic plants prefer, but if the water is in shade it should be kept chemically clear, with perhaps a fountain to ripple the surface. Hemerocallis, hosta and bergenia would be appropriate planted in the pebbles near the pool, although they will thrive equally in other parts of the garden.

A further combination of shingle and paving is illustrated in plan 8, which also incorporates a small lawn. The design focuses on the circle of bricks infilled with pebbles, and paving links the house to the workshop.

Apart from their aesthetic merits, pebbles are a relatively economical material and the labour involved is minimal. They are also very adaptable. In problem areas where the ground stays very wet in winter but dries up in summer, making weeds difficult to control, an attractive solution is to simulate an old river bed by strewing pebbles and boulders on the surface. There are many plants suitable for this situation, including *Cornus alba* 'Elegantissima', *C.alba* 'Spaethii', *Arundinaria nitida, A. murielae,* cultivars of *Miscanthus sinensis, Filipendula purpurea, Iris sibirica, I. foetidissima, Bergenia* hybrids and *Geranium macrorrhizum.* In shady places many ferns will tolerate a degree of dryness in summer, provided the roots are cool, and they look completely natural with fronds fanning out from under the larger rocks.

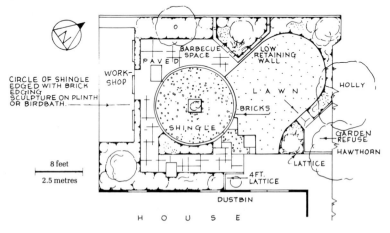

Plan 8: an alternative to a large lawn, with about two thirds of the garden under hard surfaces

A herb garden

Many of the old familiar flowers of our gardens could find a legitimate place in the herb garden. They were credited with curative, cosmetic and other powers in the past, recalled in common names like Cupid's dart and feverfew, and are not only of historical interest but often colourful and decorative plants. However, most people planning a herb garden today will concentrate on culinary herbs like thyme and parsley, perhaps adding a few others such as rue or balm for authenticity and effect. Grown in their own special area instead of relegated to a corner of the vegetable patch, herbs can become a delightful feature of the garden. Generally speaking, they thrive in any ordinary soil that is well drained but fairly moist and preferably in a light and sunny situation. It is sensible to keep mint, parsley, chives and others in everyday use within easy reach of the kitchen, but there is no reason why these should not be repeated in the herb garden itself.

The first requirements are to determine the amount of space available and to select the herbs one wishes to grow. There are various possible layouts. A circular garden with beds separated by paths radiating from the centre like the spokes of a cartwheel is attractive, but has the disadvantage that the narrow wedge-shaped sections offer very limited planting space. A rectangular design may be more practical. On a small scale, a simple method is to place paving stones 2 feet square (60 × 60 cm) with the corners just touching, forming a chequered pattern with alternate planting pockets, as illustrated in plan 9. The paving gives structural substance to the planting scheme, provides paths for walking among and picking the herbs and integrates the herb garden with the terrace or patio. Tall-growing fennel, tarragon and angelica would not be suitable for such a garden and are better grown elsewhere, perhaps in a mixed border with herbaceous plants, but many of the smaller herbs like chives, parsley and savory could be fitted into these compartments, together with a few pot marigolds for a touch of colour among the mauves, blues and whites.

A design on a larger scale is represented in plan 10 (overleaf), a herb garden measuring 60 × 46 feet (18 × 13.8 m), with room for a great variety of plants. This garden within a garden is completely enclosed except for the two gates, to create a feeling of seclusion and tranquillity and the illusion that we are taking a step back in

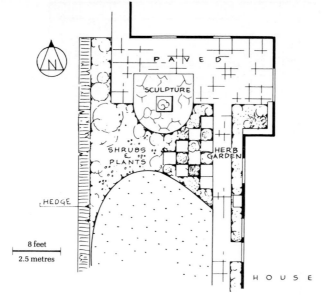

Plan 9: a herb garden incorporated in a small garden

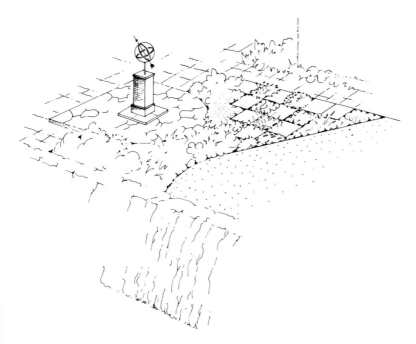

Sketch of the garden in plan 9

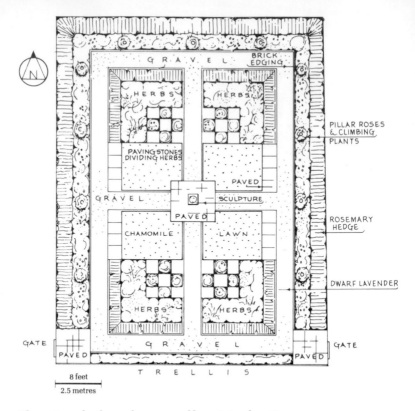

Plan 10: a herb garden as a self-contained entity

time. Hedges or trellis may be used, or a combination of the two, as shown on the plan. English yew, box or, on well drained soil, rosemary make good hedges, but trellis has much to recommend it, since it takes up less space and is not so time-consuming to maintain. It can also provide support for scented climbing plants and roses. The garden is large enough to contain a wide assortment of herbs. As well as the formal hedge of rosemary, dwarf lavender edges the four rectangular beds. The chequerboard pattern is made up as before, with five paving stones and four compartments for small plants. Taller herbs could be grown in the four L-shaped borders and need not be restricted purely to culinary sorts.

Above: a herb garden at the Chelsea Show, 1986, with compartments formed by bricks and concrete slabs

Below: a herb garden divided by hedges of dwarf box and enclosed with climbing roses

The old-fashioned *Monarda didyma*, flowering from summer to autumn, is attractive to bees

The list below is a selection of plants that qualify for a place in the herb garden because of their historical associations and ornamental value. Culinary herbs are dealt with in the Wisley handbook of that title.

Achillea millefolium (yarrow, milfoil) has been cultivated for medicinal purposes since the fifteenth century and is best in the red and pink forms; 2 feet (60 cm) high.
Anthemis nobilis (chamomile) was valued from very early times as a tonic and a cure for fever. In Tudor days it was popular for lawns.

Artemisia abrotanum (southernwood, old man, lad's love) has been recognized for its curative properties since the first century. The odour from the leaves is reputed to keep away moths, hence the intriguing French name *garde-robe* (literally wardrobe); 3 to 4 feet (90–120 cm) high.

Campanula persicifolia (peach-leafed bellflower) was an ingredient in several remedies and is very decorative with its blue flowers; 3 feet (90 cm) high.

Catananche caerulea (Cupid's dart) was formerly used in love potions and has blue flowers; 2 feet (60 cm) high.

Chrysanthemum parthenium (feverfew) has enjoyed a recent revival for its medicinal qualities, particularly the treatment of migraine, and the golden-leafed form, 'Aureum', is an excellent foliage plant with white flowers; 2 feet (60 cm) high.

Eryngium maritimum (sea holly) grows wild on our sea shores and the roots and leaves were supposed to heal many different ailments. It has attractive steely blue thistle-like flowers; 2 feet (60 cm) high.

Monarda didyma (scarlet bergamot, Oswego tea, bee balm) has scented leaves which were used for tea and brilliant scarlet flowers, showy enough to include in any planting scheme; 4 feet (1.2 m) high.

Origanum majorana (sweet majoram) was much esteemed by the ancient Greeks and has been grown in England since the fourteenth century; a well known culinary herb, it is also worth a place for its pretty sprays of mauve flowers; 2 feet (60 cm) high.

Pulmonaria officinalis (lungwort, soldiers and sailors, Jerusalem cowslip, spotted dog) was used as a pot herb in the past and believed to have numerous medicinal qualities. It has large silver-spotted leaves and pink flowers changing to blue; 6 to 9 inches (15–22 cm) high.

Tanacetum vulgare (tansy) was employed as a bitter flavouring, especially in tansy pudding, and as a remedy for various complaints. It has yellow flowers; 2 to 3 feet (60–90 cm) high.

Viola tricolor (heart's ease), our native wild pansy, has many other common names and was once considered to have excellent curative properties. Growing at random among larger plants in beds and between paving, it is most attractive and produces its purple, yellow and white or blue flowers over a long period; 3 inches (7 cm) high.

A period garden

At the beginning of the eighteenth century when Queen Anne came to the throne, the English formal garden was at its peak and the landscape movement, which would sweep away the enclosed spaces and intricate patterns of the Tudors and Stuarts, had scarcely begun. The repertoire of garden plants had also expanded and many new introductions were by then established in cultivation.

Probably introduced by the Crusaders, *Lychnis chalcedonica* does best in a sunny position (see p. 38)

A period garden of this kind is not difficult for the modern gardener to reproduce and it is a fascinating exercise for anyone interested in the evolution of gardening and the history of plants. Plan 11 is a simplified design for an imaginary garden of about 1700, containing authentic plants which would have been in cultivation at that date. Many of these are still grown unchanged today and are readily available, although others have been replaced by more recent hybrids. The planting scheme is intended to distribute specific areas of colour in different parts of the garden. (See overleaf for key to plants numbered on the plan.)

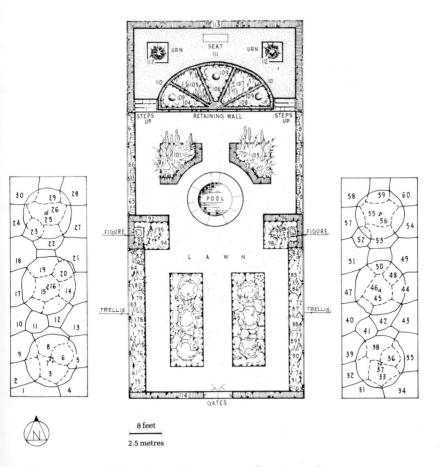

Plan 11: a period garden, with seventeenth-century plants

37

Key

Island beds

1	7	*Dianthus barbatus* (sweet William)
2	5	*Pulsatilla vulgaris* (*Anemone pulsatilla*) (pasque flower)
3	5	*Gladiolus illyricus*
4	5	*Impatiens balsamina* (balsam, touch-me-not) – summer
	15	*Narcissus × incomparabilis* – spring
5	5	*Dictamnus albus* (*D. fraxinella*) (burning bush)
6	3	*Lychnis chalcedonica* (Maltese or Jerusalem cross)
7	1	*Rosa gallica* 'Versicolor' ('Rosa Mundi')
8	3	*Saponaria officinalis* 'Albo Plena', 'Roseo Plena', 'Rubra Plena' (soapwort)
9	5	*Impatiens balsamina* – summer
	15	*Narcissus × incomparabilis* – spring
10	5	*Lychnis coronaria* (rose campion, dusty miller)
11	3	*Lilium martagon* (Turk's cap lily)
12	3	*Verbascum nigrum* (dark mullein)
13	5	*Impatiens balsamina* – summer
	15	*Narcissus × incomparabilis* – spring
14	3	*Centaurea montana* (cornflower, mountain knapweed)
15	3	*Geranium pratense* (cranesbill)
16	1	*Rosa × alba* (white rose)
17	3	*Tradescantia virginiana* (spiderwort)
18	5	*Impatiens balsamina* – summer
	15	*Narcissus × incomparabilis* – spring
19	3	*Hemerocallis flava* (daylily)
20	3	*Lilium candidum* (Madonna lily)
21	5	*Aquilegia vulgaris* (columbine)
22	3	*Asphodeline lutea* (asphodel, king's spear)
23	3	*Lychnis chalcedonica*
24	7	*Dianthus barbatus*
25	1	*Rosa gallica officinalis* (apothecaries' rose, red rose of Lancaster)
26	3	*Polemonium caeruleum* (Jacob's ladder) (see p. 41)
27	5	*Impatiens balsamina* – summer
	15	*Narcissus × incomparabilis* – spring
28	5	*Geum rivale* (water avens)
29	5	*Dianthus plumarius* (pink)
30	3	*Campanula glomerata* (bellflower)
31	5	*Aquilegia vulgaris*
32	9	*Linum arboreum* (tree flax)
33	3	*Polygonatum multiflorum* (Solomon's seal)
34	3	*Eryngium planum* (sea holly)
35	3	*Thalictrum minus* (*T. adiantifolium*) (meadow rue)
36	3	*Lilium candidum*
37	1	*Rosa gallica officinalis*
38	3	*Campanula trachelium* (throatwort)
39	5	*Impatiens balsamina* – summer
	15	*Narcissus × incomparabilis* – spring

40	3	*Centaurea montana*
41	3	*Lysimachia vulgaris* (yellow loosestrife)
42	3	*Agrimonia eupatoria* (agrimony)
43	5	*Impatiens balsamina* – summer
	15	*Narcissus* × *incomparabilis* – spring
44	3	*Origanum onites* (pot majoram)
45	5	*Gladiolus illyricus*
46	1	*Rosa* × *alba*
47	3	*Tradescantia virginiana*
48	3	*Lychnis chalcedonica*
49	3	*Centranthus ruber* (red valerian)
50	3	*Chelidonium majus* 'Flore Pleno' (greater celandine)
51	5	*Impatiens balsamina* – summer
	15	*Narcissus* × *incomparabilis* – spring
52	3	*Lilium candidum*
53	3	*Tanacetum vulgare* (tansy)
54	5	*Impatiens balsamina* – summer
	15	*Narcissus* × *incomparabilis* – spring
55	5	*Gladiolus illyricus*
56	1	*Rosa gallica* 'Versicolor'
57	1	*Aster amellus*
58	3	*Pulmonaria officinalis* (lungwort)
59	3	*Chrysanthemum parthenium* 'Aureum' (feverfew)
60	7	*Dianthus barbatus*

Planting scheme for garden layout

61	1	*Rosmarinus officinalis* (rosemary)
62	1	*Jasminum officinale* (jasmine)
63	1	*Rosmarinus officinalis*
64	1	*Clematis flammula*
65	1	*Lonicera periclymenum* (honeysuckle, woodbine)
66	1	*Rosmarinus officinalis*
67	1	*Lathyrus latifolius* (perennial pea)
68	1	*Clematis flammula*
69	1	*Rosmarinus officinalis*
70	1	*Jasminum officinale*
71	1	*Lathyrus latifolius*
72	1	*Rosmarinus officinalis*
73	1	*Lonicera periclymenum*
74	1	*Rosmarinus officinalis*
75	7	*Astrantia major* (black masterwort)
76	5	*Lilium bulbiferum croceum* (orange lily)
77	5	*Alchemilla vulgaris* (lady's mantle)
78	5	*Lilium bulbiferum croceum*
79	5	*Alchemilla vulgaris*
80	5	*Lilium bulbiferum croceum*
81	5	*Alchemilla vulgaris*
82	3	*Althaea rosea* (hollyhock)
83	25	*Lavandula angustifolia* (*L. spica*) (English lavender)
84	3	*Althaea rosea*

85	5 *Alchemilla vulgaris*
86	5 *Lilium bulbiferum croceum*
87	5 *Alchemilla vulgaris*
88	5 *Lilium bulbiferum croceum*
89	5 *Alchemilla vulgaris*
90	5 *Lilium bulbiferum croceum*
91	7 *Astrantia major*
92	14 *Phillyrea latifolia spinosa*
93	12 *Convallaria majalis* (lily-of-the-valley)
94	9 *Lamium maculatum* (spotted dead nettle)
95	1 *Yucca filamentosa* (silk grass)
96	14 *Phillyrea latifolia spinosa*
97	12 *Convallaria majalis*
98	9 *Lamium maculatum*
99	1 *Yucca filamentosa*
100	14 *Phillyrea latifolia spinosa*
101	5 *Acanthus mollis* (bear's breeches)
102	14 *Phillyrea latifolia spinosa*
103	5 *Acanthus mollis*
104	15 *Armeria maritima* (thrift)
105	6 *Canna indica* (Indian shot) – summer
	50 tulips striped or feathered – spring
106	15 *Armeria maritima*
107	6 *Canna indica* – summer
	50 tulips striped or feathered – spring
108	15 *Armeria maritima*
109	3 *Kochia scoparia trichophylla* (summer cypress)
110	120 feet (36.5 m) *Buxus sempervirens* 'Suffruticosa' (edging box)
111	30 *Anthemis nobilis* (camomile)
112	3 *Agave americana marginata* (American aloe)
	24 *Hyacinthus orientalis* (hyacinth)
113	60 *Taxus baccata* (English yew)
114	30 *Taxus baccata*

Interplanting for island beds in vacant spaces

Lysimachia nummularia (creeping Jenny, moneywort)
Viola tricolor (heart's ease)
Meconopsis cambrica (Welsh poppy)
Hieracium aurantiacum (orange hawkweed)
Geranium phaeum (mourning widow)
Iberis umbellata (candytuft) – seed

Above: *Polemonium caeruleum*, contributing a cool blue in early summer, has been grown since Roman times

Below: *Meconopsis cambrica*, a native of Britain, produces its brilliant flowers in late spring

Making a ha-ha

The landscape movement which became so fashionable in the eighteenth century was based on the principle that the garden should merge with the surrounding countryside to form a single panoramic picture, including perhaps a man-made lake, a Grecian temple, groups of trees nestling in the folds of distant hills and livestock grazing near the house without any visible boundary fence. The picture was, of course, an illusion brought about by the ha-ha, a broad steep ditch which does not impede the view.

However, the use of the ha-ha need not be confined to large estates such as those created by Lancelot 'Capability' Brown. It can be extremely effective in a garden of moderate size in a space only about 40 feet (12 m) wide. The first consideration is drainage, which will be influenced by the texture of the soil and the lie of the land, and there should be adequate provision for piping away any

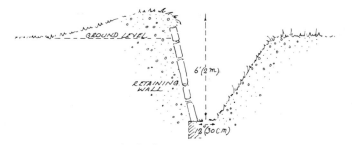

Figure 4: cross-section of a ha-ha

Sketch showing position of ha-ha

Above: a ha-ha viewed from the 'visible' side, with the retaining wall

Below: *Osmanthus × burkwoodii*, a useful hardy evergreen shrub with fragrant flowers in April and May (see p. 44)

water that might collect in the bottom of the trench. Originally, when labour and materials were cheap, a ha-ha might be dug as deep as 8 feet (2.4 m), but 5 to 6 feet (1.5–1.8 m) should be sufficient, depending on the animals to be kept in the pasture (see figure 4, p. 42). The flat bottom of the trench should be 1 foot (30 cm) wide and a retaining wall should be built up the steeper side, ensuring that holes are made towards the base for drainage. This wall can be constructed of bricks or stone or old railway sleepers, although the latter are not very attractive. Concrete walling blocks are relatively inexpensive and weather quickly, becoming covered with moss and lichen on a north-facing surface. The bank opposite the wall should be turfed.

It is a great help if the ha-ha can be placed where the land falls away from the viewpoint towards the open country. One can then dig into the slope and spread surplus soil over the higher ground in front of the ha-ha to raise the height of the wall. Groups of evergreen shrubs and medium-sized conifers planted at each end of the ha-ha will frame the view. Suitable shrubs would be *Osmanthus × burkwoodii*, *Stranvaesia davidiana*, *Cotoneaster lacteus*, *C.* 'Cornubia', *Elaeagnus × ebbingei* and *Viburnum rhytidophyllum*. It goes without saying that the lawn should flow towards the top of the wall of the ha-ha without interruption.

A sunken fence is another way to achieve an invisible boundary and requires less excavation (see figure 5). A trench is dug 4 feet (1.2 m) deep with sloping sides. The width should be 10 feet (3 m) at the top and 3 feet (90 cm) at the bottom and a post-and-wire fence is erected along the middle of the trench below eye-level.

Figure 5:   a sunken fence

A heather garden

One could probably say without exaggeration that heathers contribute more colour throughout the year than any other group of plants and the relatively short gap between the end of April and the end of June, when they are not in flower, is bridged by those with golden or bronze foliage. Most heathers require a lime-free soil, although Erica herbacea (E. carnea) and E. × darleyensis are happy enough except on very thin chalky soils, giving us some of the best winter colour from November to April (see also the Wisley handbook, Heaths and heathers).

There are several ways to make a heather garden, one of the deciding factors being the space available. However, even a few square yards is sufficient for a varied collection interplanted with dwarf conifers. Whether planting in hundreds or in small numbers, rewarding results can be expected for very little work. The beautiful heather gardens at Kew, Edinburgh and the RHS Garden, Wisley, are laid out on a grander scale than most of us could imagine in our own gardens, but much can be learned from the principles on which they are designed. Heathers should be planted 1 to $1\frac{1}{4}$ feet (30–37 cm) apart, in groups of at least three to five of the same sort; single plants are never effective. These drifts can be allowed to overlap where they meet for a less contrived appearance.

Unless one is prepared to do some propagating from a small nucleus of plants, even a modest heather garden can be costly to stock. Fortunately, heathers are fairly easy to raise from cuttings and will develop into good flowering plants within little more than a year. Another economical method is to reduce the number of heathers by choosing suitable conifers and shrubs to complement them and fill up spaces in the beds. Juniperus communis 'Repanda', which makes a green rug-like carpet, and J. communis 'Hornibrookii', with grey-green foliage spreading in all directions to follow the contours of the ground, can both be recommended. They will cover an area 10 to 12 feet (3–3.6 m) across – equivalent to about 50 heathers. Cotoneaster dammeri, an evergreen shrub with red berries, is completely prostrate and extends indefinitely over the ground, though it is easily controlled. Rubus calycinoides forms dense widespreading mats of evergreen glossy leaves with white flowers.

A new heather garden often looks bare and sparsely planted

45

Left: a small bed of heathers and dwarf conifers against a background of shrubs

Right: the leaves and flowers of *Anaphalis triplinervis* 'Summer Snow' make an attractive foil for heathers

before the heathers and shrubs have grown together and become established. One solution is to cover the soil with a layer of moist coarse peat or forest bark, which provides an attractive foil for the plants. However, it must be emphasized that the mulch and the soil should be thoroughly moist before application, otherwise the shrubs might suffer from lack of water.

A place for *Hamamelis mollis* should be found in the heather garden. With its bright yellow flowers and upright branches, it is an ideal shrub for underplanting with *Erica herbacea* 'King George' ('Winter Beauty'), to provide one of the finest examples of winter colour from December to February. (See also *Heaths and heathers* for further suggestions of shrub and conifers to use with heathers.)

The planting schemes illustrated in plan 12 are for island beds, but they can be adapted to fit in with other shapes and with the overall design of the garden concerned. If the beds are divided by grass paths, for instance, some of the plants can be repeated on each side.

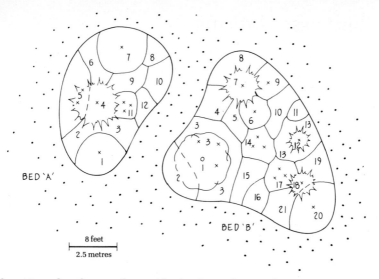

Plan 12:   a heather garden, with shrubs and groundcover

Key

Bed A

1	1	*Juniperus communis* 'Repanda'
2	9	*Calluna vulgaris* 'Tib'
3	10	*Erica herbacea* 'King George' ('Winter Beauty')
4	1	*Chamaecyparis pisifera* 'Filifera Aurea'
5	2	*Rubus calycinoides*
6	9	*Erica vagans* 'Mrs D. F. Maxwell'
7	1	*Erica arborea alpina*
8	5	*Erica herbacea* 'King George'
9	9	*Calluna vulgaris* 'Alportii'
10	5	*Stachys* 'Silver Carpet'
11	3	*Helictotrichon sempervirens*
12	7	*Erica vagans* 'Mrs D. F. Maxwell'

Bed B

1	1	*Hamamelis mollis*
2	10	*Erica herbacea* 'King George'
3	3	*Cotoneaster dammeri*

4	7	*Calluna vulgaris* 'Mair's Variety'
5	7	*Calluna vulgaris* 'J. H. Hamilton'
6	1	*Cistus* 'Silver Pink'
7	1	*Chamaecyparis pisifera* 'Boulevard'
8	7	*Polygonum vacciniifolium*
9	1	*Juniperus sabina* 'Tamariscifolia'
10	9	*Calluna vulgaris* 'Peter Sparkes'
11	3	*Anaphalis triplinervis*
12	1	*Thuja orientalis* 'Aurea Nana'
13	15	*Erica herbacea* 'King George'
14	3	*Ceratostigma willmottianum*
15	9	*Erica × darleyensis*
16	5	*Calluna vulgaris* 'Golden Feather'
17	3	*Helictotrichon sempervirens*
18	1	*Chamaecyparis lawsoniana* 'Ellwoodii'
19	12	*Erica vagans* 'St Keverne'
20	1	*Genista lydia*

47

Plant associations

The effectiveness of a particular plant is greatly enhanced if it is placed with an eye to the harmonizing colours or different foliage shapes of its neighbours, for example the silvery fern-like acaena combined with burgundy-coloured ajuga, or the reed-like foliage of miscanthus or yucca set off by the large rounded leaves of bergenia.

In the rock garden, shrub border or heather garden, the contrasting outline of a narrow upright conifer behind the low horizontal branches of junipers has a more lasting visual impact than any flower, which compensates to some extent for the lack of blossom and scent. On a larger scale, extravagantly weeping deciduous trees, such as *Betula pendula* 'Youngii' and *Prunus × yedoensis* 'Ivensii' (sometimes described as weeping like a crinoline), are seen at their best in winter and spring near the vertical columns of blue-grey conifers (see p. 51).

The following suggestions for grouping plants continue those given in *Plans for small gardens*. They include trees that can be planted sufficiently wide apart to make specimens, but close enough to be viewed in the same context, although this arrangement requires a fairly large amount of space. The trees have been chosen not for their flowers, which make a relatively brief contribution, but for the colours of their leaves, stems or barks.

Trees

Pyrus salicifolia 'Pendula'; *Prunus spinosa* 'Purpurea'; and *Gleditsia triacanthos* 'Sunburst'. Colours: silver; deep purple; and gold foliage. Summer.

Acer negundo 'Variegatum'; and *Prunus cerasifera* 'Pissardii'. Colours: leaves with irregular white margins; and dark red turning to purple. Summer.

Acer platanoides 'Drummondii'; and *A. platanoides* 'Crimson King'. Colours: leaves with a marginal white band; and deep crimson-purple. Summer.

Sorbus aria; and *Taxus baccata*. Colours: greyish green and white; and deep green leaves. Summer.

Salix alba 'Sericea'; and *Corylus maxima* 'Purpurea'. Colours: bright silvery; and deep purple leaves. Summer.

Betula pendula (deciduous); *Pinus sylvestris* (evergreen); and *Larix kaempferi* (deciduous). Colours: white stems; reddish young bark with blue-green leaves; and reddish purple twigs. Planted as a belt of trees, the silver birch, Scots pine and Japanese larch produce some of the most beautiful winter colour in the landscape.

Shrubs, perennials and grasses

Potentilla 'Elizabeth'; *Ceratostigma willmottianum*; and *Ruta graveolens* 'Jackman's Blue'. Colours: primrose yellow; and plumbago blue flowers; blue-grey foliage. May to October.

Cotoneaster horizontalis; and *Euonymus fortunei* 'Silver Queen'. Colours: red berries; and creamy yellow variegated leaves. Autumn and early winter (see p. 50).

Berberis thunbergii atropurpurea; and *Phlomis fruticosa*. Colours: purple foliage; and grey felted leaves with spikes of yellow flowers. June and July.

Viburnum × bodnantense 'Dawn', with small spring bulbs. Colours: pink flowers. November to February.

Cortaderia selloana 'Pumila'; and *Rhus typhina* 'Laciniata'. Colours: feathery silver plumes; and fern-like orange and yellow leaves. Autumn.

Evergreen azaleas and rhododendrons with *Lilium hansonii, L. henryi, L. regale* and forms of *L. speciosum*. Colours: mixed. May to July.

Helictotrichon sempervirens with heathers. Colours: Glaucous-blue arching foliage and various flower and leaf colours. Summer and winter.

Cornus alba 'Elegantissima'; and *Clematis × jackmanii*. Colours: greyish green leaves with silver edges; and blue flowers. July and August.

Thuja occidentalis 'Rheingold'; and *Erica herbacea* 'King George'. Colours: Rich old gold foliage; and rose pink flowers. November to February.

Iris foetidissima; and *Bergenia cordifolia*. Colours: sword-like leaves with orange fruit; and large roundish deep green leaves. December to February.

Above: the rich autumn colour of *Cotoneaster horizontalis* (left) associates well with the variegated foliage of *Euonymus fortunei* 'Silver Queen' (right); both may be grown against a wall

Below: daylilies like *Hemerocallis* 'Burning Daylight' (left) combine pleasantly with the popular *Ceanothus* 'Gloire de Versailles' (right)

Corokia cotoneaster with ericas and callunas. Colours: small dainty leaves with yellow starry flowers and various. May, winter to summer for heathers.

Hydrangeas; and *Hemerocallis* 'Burning Daylight'. Colours: blue; and glowing orange flowers. July to September.

Hippophae rhamnoides; and *Cotinus coggygria* 'Royal Purple'. Colours: narrow silver leaves with orange berries; and deep purple leaves. Summer and autumn.

Ceanothus 'Gloire de Versailles'; and various hemerocallis. Colours: blue; and pink, crimson or yellow flowers. June to October.

Young's weeping birch, *Betula pendula* 'Youngii', set off by the contrasting shapes and colours of conifers

Scent in the garden

While a camellia or a nerine is bound to be admired for its elegance or beauty, even the most demure and humble flower is cherished if it can offer scent. Mignonette and lily-of-the-valley, for example, would probably not receive a second glance were it not for the fragrance of their flowers. There are many more scented plants than can be mentioned here, but my purpose is to select a few shrubs that are valuable for their perfume, most of them deservedly popular for this very reason.

Many of the shrubs which are appreciated for winter-flowering have the bonus of fragrant blossom. This certainly applies to *Viburnum × bodnantense* 'Dawn', which bears sprays of richly scented pink flowers from November until February, interrupted only by the severest weather. The Chinese witch-hazel, *Hamamelis mollis*, has already been recommended (see p. 46). Its delicious perfume on one of those fleeting but precious sunny days we sometimes experience in January helps to make up for the bleakness of winter and the clusters of golden yellow strap-like flowers seem oblivious to frost and snow. The fragrant parchment-like blooms of the winter sweet, *Chimonanthus praecox*, pale yellow stained purple at the centre, are a joy to see in December and January, although this shrub is relatively uncommon, perhaps because it does not flower until it is established. The cultivar 'Luteus' has slightly larger flowers of a uniform waxy yellow, opening a little later, but is equally fragrant.

A shrubby honeysuckle, *Lonicera × purpusii*, contributes winter blossom and scent with freely borne creamy white flowers in January and February. It can be trained against a low wall so that the perfume may be savoured near the house. The sarcococcas are useful low-growing evergreens, with small white flowers opening in late winter. Though modest, these are scented and the bluish green willow-like foliage combines well with paving and stone. They will grow in shady places that are not too dry and *S.humilis* makes good ground cover.

Above: *Hamamelis mollis*, one of the most valuable winter-flowering shrubs, bearing fragrant blooms from December to March

Below: the charming mezereon, *Daphne mezereum*, a small deciduous shrub which flourishes on chalky soils (see p. 53)

As spring approaches, *Mahonia japonica* offers some of the best scented blossom of the year, producing clusters of lemon-coloured flowers in long racemes from February to early March above bold, leathery, soft green foliage. Properly placed, it is a fine feature, but lacks the imposing upright habit of other mahonias which are so useful in garden design. At the same time of year, the exquisite perfume of *Daphne mezereum* cannot be ignored and the clustered, wax-like, reddish purple flowers on leafless stems are a beautiful sight, particularly when seen above a blanket of pure white snow, which is not an unusual occurrence in March. Other daphnes, *D.* 'Somerset', *D. collina* and *D. retusa*, make their presence equally known in May, with blooms in shades of pink and purple. One of the most powerfully fragrant shrubs is *Viburnum × juddii*, which is in full blossom at the end of April with rounded heads of white-flushed pink flowers.

The garden would seem incomplete without the perfume of the lilac. The many cultivars of *Syringa vulgaris*, ranging in colour from white to red, blue or purple, are a delight from May into June. Azaleas, rhododendrons and tree heaths, with their heady scent from April to June, would be an important part of a scented garden, although it must be remembered that these require acid soils.

The mock orange is reminiscent of long warm days in June, when its fragrance mingles with the smells of a summer garden. Two hybrids of moderate size suitable for a smaller garden are *Philadelphus* 'Beauclerk' and *P.* 'Silver Showers'. The Mount Etna broom, *Genista aetnensis*, is a graceful shrub with golden yellow scented flowers on almost leafless thread-like branches in July. In planting schemes it provides a light and airy tallness up to 18 feet (5.4 m) high without casting shade. The Spanish broom, *Spartium junceum*, is closely related but more bushy and twiggy. Unlike most brooms, it holds its very fragrant flowers over a long period, from June to September.

Gardens of different shapes and sizes

TWO NARROW GARDENS MERGED IN ONE

In plan 13 (p. 58) two narrow adjoining gardens are united in one, the plot on the right being 1 foot (30 cm) lower than the other. The split in levels contributes useful features to the design, necessitating a limited amount of structural stonework, with steps leading down from the new pergola and sufficient walling to make a flat area for the patio and a small lawn. Elsewhere the different levels are absorbed into the borders adjacent to the path.

The outline of the garden invites a way of approach from various directions. The position of the pergola is governed by an existing grapevine and fortuitously allows it to be placed at an angle.

A MEDIUM-SIZED GARDEN OF UNUSUAL SHAPE

Plan 14 (p. 59) demonstrates different requirements in a triangular garden of medium size. It includes a naturalized area and small hazel coppice, a summerhouse, beds for shrub roses, herbaceous perennials and dahlias, flowering and berrying shrubs, a rock garden, a plot for vegetables and fruit and a greenhouse.
shrubs and trees have been discarded. The ones specified on the plan were considered to contribute to the reconstruction of the garden.

A GREENHOUSE AS A FEATURE

The hexagonal greenhouse can be an attractive feature in its own right, but is even better if integrated with the design of the garden.

Overleaf above: a rock garden planted with undemanding alpines, including aubrieta, saxifrage and iberis

Below: an alternative to the rectangular lawn, flanked by mixed borders and rising to a pool at the end

Page 57 above: imaginative use of crazy paving in curves and steps

Below: paving is a feature of many gardens, old and new, and can be very decorative

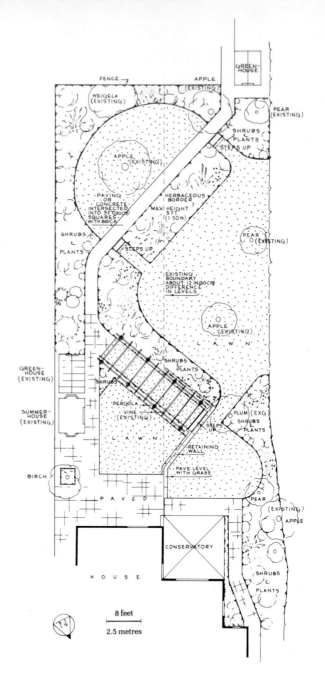

Plan 13:   two narrow gardens in one

58

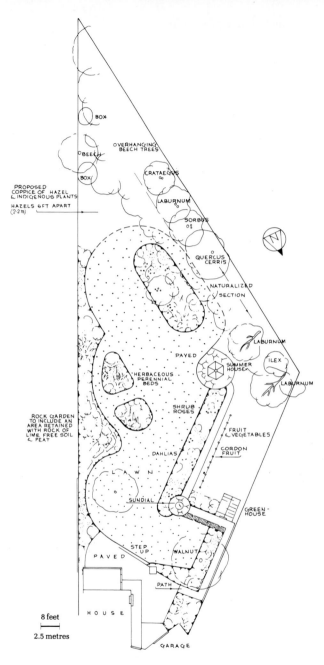

Plan 14: a medium-sized garden of unusual shape

Plan 15: a garden including a greenhouse

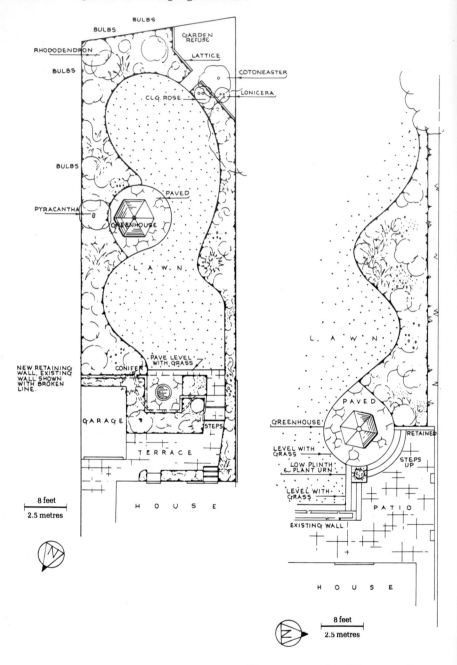

Plan 16: a patio with a greenhouse

In this respect plans 15 and 16 are basically similar. One shows a complete garden with existing trees and shrubs and the other illustrates a corner of a garden specifically intended to combine the greenhouse with the planting scheme and patio. In both cases, the area surrounding the greenhouse has been laid out in a similar manner, except the reverse way round.

A VERY SMALL GARDEN INCORPORATING A LAWN

The garden in plan 17 measures less than 48 feet (14.4 m) by 18 feet (5.4 m). The idea is to introduce an alternative to the rectangular lawn by creating one of irregular shape bordered by a narrow bed,

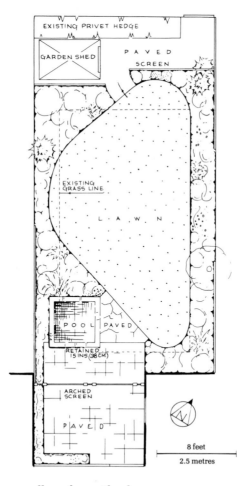

Plan 17: a very small garden with a lawn

or what might be described as a lawn with a fringe. It is an example of how a lawn can be included satisfactorily in a very small space, where it is important that outlines should be continuous and not broken up with little curves. The raised pool is situated near the house and patio, so that aquatic plants and life can be observed from there.

INTRODUCING CURVES TO ADD SPACE

Curves in a small garden 60 by 34 feet (18 by 10.2 m) increase the visual impression that the garden is larger than it really is. In plan 18 the line of paving and of the beds flows without interruption and there are two focal points – the urn on the left and a small conifer on the right at the widest point of the border, which balances a view of the ornamental tree on the lawn.

There is a choice of material for the patio. Crazy paving can be fitted easily into a curve, but is a little more difficult to lay than reconstituted stone, which is made in fixed sizes and thicknesses and can be cut to the required shape with a masonry saw.

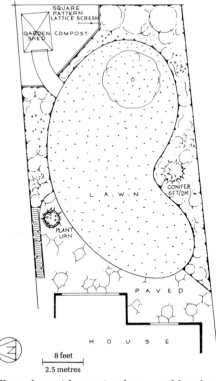

Plan 18: a small garden with curving lawn and borders

CREATING VISTAS

The layout of the garden in plan 19 creates unimpeded views by using the maximum amount of space available. The major emphasis lies towards the right, with the bird bath and conifer on each side of a broad grass inlet. The circle of bricks is centralized

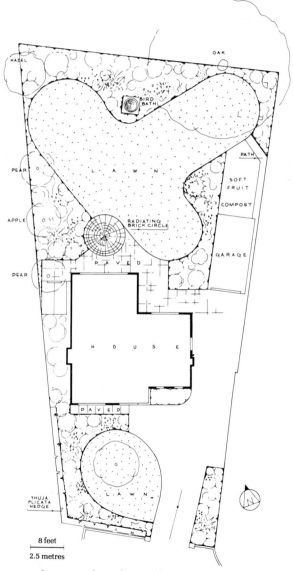

Plan 19: a medium-sized garden with vistas

on the door to the garden and makes an attractive contrast to the shape and colour of the patio. It could equally well be constructed with concrete setts, which adapt so easily to form curved patterns and circles.

The garage intrudes into the garden, but the three directional design detracts from its presence. At the front of the house, the lawn has an unbroken outline to complement a small specimen tree and is flanked by shrubs providing interest and colour throughout the year. Shrubs and trees planted by the previous owners are shown on the plan.